To Mom
with best wishes
and much love

B.G. & J

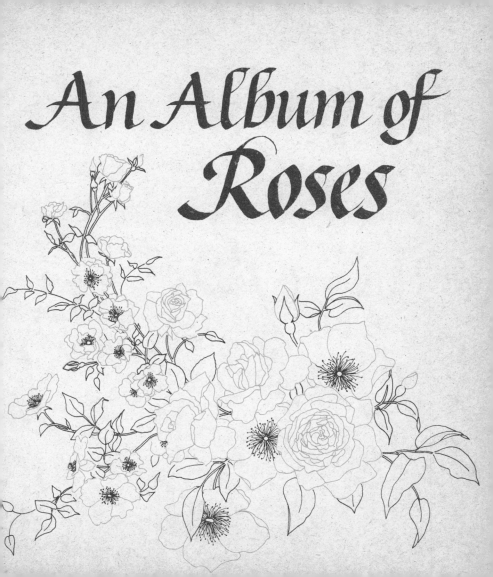

An Album of
Roses

An Album of Roses

Compiled by
Nancy Dunnan
Phoebe Phillips

Illustrated by
Julia Morland

Calligraphy by
Dorothy Avery

Designers:
Lorraine Johnson
Danny Robins

The Viking Press New York

An Album of Roses
Phoebe Phillips / Nancy Dunnan
Copyright.© Phoebe Phillips & Nancy Dunnan
1978

Published in 1978 by The Viking Press
625, Madison Avenue, New York, N.Y. 10022
Published simultaneously in Canada by
Penguin Books Canada Ltd.

Library of Congress Cataloging in
Publication Data

Phillips, Phoebe
    An Album of Roses
    I. Roses 1. Dunnan, Nancy
        Joint Author
    II. S.B.411.P47   63 9/33/372 78/1538
    JSBN 0-670-11187-2

Printed in the United States of America

This book is dedicated to
everyone everywhere
who loves roses

CONTENTS

THE FIRST ROSES

Oh, no man knows
Through what wild
centuries
Roves back the rose.

Walter de la Mare

The story of the very first rose remains clouded by legend, although fossils found in Europe, Japan and America are some 35 million years old. But the very first pictorial evidence we have is a six petalled flower on a heavily restored fresco at Knossos in Crete, dating back to 1500 B.C.

Five hundred years later, wild roses were brought back as precious spoils of war by King Sargon's campaigners from the city of Ur. In Greece, Homer wrote about roses on Achilles' shield, and three centuries later, Sappho of Lesbos called them Queen of flowers.

SAPPHO'S FLOWERS

But roses fade, and summer's sun will end,
    And oaths be broken.
So never swear to love. Or if you do,
Remember oaths can make no rose eternal,
Nor keep the sun from setting, nor bestow
    A second summer!

Her beauty is like the roses that are gay
    with perfume, And shining.

Gold is god, immortal,
That keeps its lustre ever.
The lovely rose shall wither,
And age shall take our bodies
Our bodies like the roses
By mortals are engendered.

    Sappho, trans. Saklatvala.

The Mediterranian world in the Classical period was rose mad; the volcanic island of Rhodes took the flower for its emblem and its name (Greek rhodon) and the mainland exported huge quantities of fresh flowers to Cleopatra's luxurious court in Alexandria, where petals were thickly strewn over palace floors. At one banquet for Mark Antony the carpet of petals was 18 inches thick.

The Egyptians soon established their own nurseries to supply the Roman aristocracy with garlands and the ingredients for rose flavored jellies and puddings and rosewater. Nero paid four million sesterces for one evening's floral decoration. A disapproving Cicero wrote that banquets were served to guests on rose covered couches. Virgil was less critical—he loved the famous rose garden at Paestrum, and Pliny wrote about the fountains running with rosewater for special occasions, and he also listed the twelve best known roses of his time.

PLINY'S LIST

Rose of Praeneste	Provence rose
Rose of Campania	Rosa alba; Virgil called this rose "Biferique rosaria Paesti" or the twice bearing rose
Rose of Miletus	Rosa gallica of Linnaeus; with no more than 12 petals
Rose of Trachyn	Rose of France, also known as Rosa rubello
Rose of Alabanda	The Eglantine rose
Spiniola rose	The thorn rose Rosa myriacantha
Rosa centifolia	
The Grecian rose	The Greek Lychnis rose, probably a garden flower, the Agrostemma coronaria
Rosa Graecula	Rosa silvestris
Rose of Macetum	The Macedonian rose. May be a variety of Alcaea rosa
Rosa Coroniola	The Rosa canina or dog rose
Rose of Cyrenae	Rosa Damascena

MYTHS AND LEGENDS

> It was roses, roses
> all the way.
>
> R. Browning

Legend and roses are inextricably tangled in mythical history. The Greeks believed that the first rose was created by the Goddess Cybele in a fit of jealousy, to ensure that there would be something on Earth more beautiful than her hated rival, Aphrodite. The Roman storytellers pictured the red rose as a reflection of the blushing Venus when Jupiter saw her bathing:

> Then, then, in strange eventful hour,
> The earth produced an infant flower,
> Which sprung with blushing tinctures rest
> And wantoned o'er its parent's breast.
> The gods beheld this brilliant birth
> And hailed the Rose, the boon of Earth.
>
> Anacreon, trans. T. Moore

Another classical legend says that when Venus ran through

a rose hedge to meet the wounded Adonis, her blood stained the flowers for all eternity.

Later, when Christianity began to re-interpret the old myths, the white rose turning to red was the perfect symbol of purity and passion. One story says that the burning logs around an early martyr's body were turned to red roses, another recalls the more sensual pagan imagery, and says it was Eve who gave us the red rose, for when she kissed the white flower in the Garden of Eden, it blushed deep pink with pleasure.

ROSES AND THE CHURCH

As Christianity began to grow, the pagan rose was officially ignored, perhaps because of its association with heady sensuality. Secretly, however, the rose was used by Christians on catacomb walls as a code for their faith, with red symbolizing the blood of the martyrs, and white the purity of Christ, Aphrodite's love-blossom transformed into a symbol of innocence. By the 5th century, Christian legends began to include the rose. Saint Ambrose wrote that in Paradise the rose had smooth stems until the Fall of Man, after which thorns appeared to remind man of his wrong-doing.

The Blessed Virgin Mary's roses remained thorn-less, however, because she herself was without thorns, free from original sin. Medieval and Renaissance paintings often show Mary in rose gardens, with rose bouquets or crowns. The rosary, actually a wreath of prayers, may take its name from the custom of offering Her rose wreaths, although in another legend, the name is derived from the prayers of a devout monk, whose words turned into roses as he spoke. Rose patterns appeared increasingly in Church architecture, most spectacularly in the

famous rose windows of Gothic cathedrals.

Most people associate St. Francis with animals but his warm love of nature embraced all flowers and roses in particular, which grew where drops of his blood fell to earth.

St. Rose of Lima was the first American to be declared a saint, in 1671; she took the name Rosa de Santa Maria and she wore a crown of rose thorns under her habit. Pope Clement X named her patron of South America, and on her feast day, roses decorate the churches in her memory.

The unique papal custom of giving golden roses began in 1049 and fashionable goldsmiths in the 14th and 15th centuries made many lovely examples. Originally they were single flowers made of red-tinted gold, but gradually the gifts became more and more ornate, set as bouquets on tall golden stands, and decorated with brilliant gems. According to Pope Alexander III, the rose symbolized Christ the King – the gold for His kingship, the red for His passion. Presented to important ecclesiastical bodies, to prominent Roman Catholics, to cities, churches and princes, the jewels were blessed on what has come to be known as Rose Sunday.

Whit Sunday was called Rose Easter in medieval England, perhaps because there were so many roses in bloom at that time. Or the name may stem from the Greek and Roman custom of planting rose bushes on graves on May 11, the day commemorating the dead, known as "dies rosae".

A FEW RECIPES

To make rose wine in the Roman fashion, Pliny sayeth:

"A weight of 40 dinirs (five ounces) of Rose leaves well stamped, put them into a linen cloth together with a little weight that they may settle downwards and not float about. Let them hang thus in 20 sextars (three gallons) and 2 Wine Quarts of Must (unfermented grape juice). Keep the vessel close stoped for 3 Months, then open it and strain the said floures into the Liquor."

A more modern version is the Italian Rossolio. Rossolio's history goes back to Elizabethan times when rosa solis was described by Pepys in his diary. He wrote about a certain Captain Ferrers drunk with rossolio, who leaped from a second-storey balcony. "The desperatest frolic I ever did see."

A Modern Rossolio

Gather one two-gallon bucket of rose petals, preferably heavily scented Damask petals or those from old fashioned roses. Pick them over carefully. Place petals in a large china or glazed earthenware crock. (A pyrex oven-proof glass container will also work.) Cover with freshly boiled water. Let petals infuse for six hours, or even overnight. Strain off the water into a clean crock or soup tureen.

For every pint of rose liquid add ½ pint of vodka which has been flavored with 1 teaspoon of cinnamon, dissolved in 1 Tablespoon of hot water. Sweeten to taste with a little sugar syrup plus a small amount of orange blossom syrup. Cork and bottle in the usual manner.

Rose hips, the fruit of the wild rose, have a particularly high vitamin C content and for centuries have been used to make a herbal tea. Sometimes rose hips were cooked in fruit pies or in a dish with mushrooms but primarily they were prized for their medicinal qualities, for as Gerarde tells us, "roses comfort a weak stomacke."

Rose Hip Tea

To make tea from rose hips, they should preferably be gathered after the first frost has touched them, when they will be slightly soft to the touch. If they must be collected earlier, choose those that are fully mature, plump, and a good color. They should be crushed with a pestle or heavy rolling pin or ground in a domestic grinder. Do not bring rose hips into contact with any metal except stainless steel, for they will lose their color and the precious store of vitamin C will be depleted. The tea is made by by soaking 4 tablespoonfuls of the crushed hips in 5 pints of water for 24 hours. Then simmer gently for half an hour but do not boil. Strain and store the liquid in covered earthenware jars or darkened bottles. When required for use, boil the quantity needed, adding dried rose hips and discarding them before drinking. Sweeten with honey.

Rose Petal Jam

2 cups dark red rose petals	4 cups sugar
1 Tablespoon sugar	¾ cup water
2 Tablespoons lemon juice	1 Tablespoon lemon juice

Rose petal jam, often served inside folded thin pancakes, is a classic dessert in the Middle East. Choose roses with a fine aroma, and pick after the dew has dried. Cut off the the yellow bases. Sprinkle with sugar and lemon juice, then crush down to reduce the bulk. Measure the petals by packing into a cup. Combine sugar and water in a kettle, bring to a boil. Add petals, and stirring frequently, simmer for about ten minutes. Add lemon juice, then leave for twelve hours. Bring to the boil again and simmer until syrup is thick and clear. Pack into jars, seal, and store in a cool dark place.

A ROYAL ROSARIAN

> I have a garden of my own
> But so with roses overgrown
> And lilies, that you would
> it guess
> To be a little wilderness.
>
> Andrew Marvell

Empress Josephine is remembered best for her clothes and her beauty, but she was also an ardent and serious lover of many flowers, and of the rose in particular. Napoleon bought her the Château Malmaison in Paris, where she created a famous garden. Her plant collectors travelled with the French army to gather unusual species, and the navy's ships often carried her gardeners, cosseting their precious discoveries in boxes to protect them from the salt spray. During the worst Anglo-French battles, her head gardener from Kew Gardens would be given a pass so that he could go freely from London to Paris to care for her plants. Pierre-Joseph Redouté, the great

Belgian painter, made over 700 studies of the 250 varieties at Malmaison. Even Napoleon's indifference to flowers was overcome by the beauty of Malmaison. Josephine lived there after their divorce until she died in 1814, and Napoleon himself chose to spend his last night at the Château before going into exile on Elba.

MAKING A ROSE GARDEN

A root in the right soil,
Sun, rain, and a man's toil;
That, as a wise man knows,
Is all there is to a rose.

O. Mackenzie

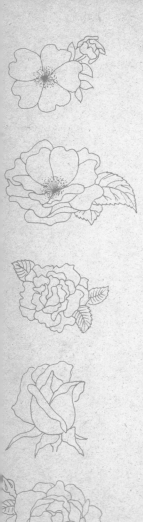

Not least among the virtues of the rose is its ability to suit any kind of gardening and to survive somehow in almost any climate. There are nearly 150 recognized species of roses common to the Northern Hemisphere and although it is not found wild in the Southern Hemisphere, it has successfully been introduced to Australia, New Zealand, and S. America.

Choose carefully according to your area and your personal preferences. The design can be Victorian formal bedding, or simple winding brick paths, with shrub roses spilling generously over the edges and scenting the air with heavy perfume.

The first thing to consider is the outside of your house, its style and situation. Natural stone and white frame houses usually look best with informal shrubs planted in country garden profusion - ramblers on the wall, climbers on the fence and an overwhelming feeling of abundance.

Town houses look attractive with heavy blooming, brightly shaded hybrids with just one or two taller varieties for emphasis. Where space is limited, don't forget walls; create them if necessary with trellis work, screen walling and fences. Do remember to build sturdily, for many climbing roses are remarkably floriferous and become extremely heavy. They should be tied on to wires or vine eyes sunk into the walls.

If you have a tall house or tree, you can grow Rosa filipes kiftsgate. This magnificent climber rises to heights of 40 feet or more, the flowers cascading in a lovely yellow waterfall.

In the city, avoid using the larger shrubs. Along narrow paths clothing catches easily on their thorns. Some of the smaller varieties are quite appropriate, but keep them pruned back.

Country gardens have a natural affinity with every kind of rose. Choice is conditioned by what pleases you, and whether your climate pleases the roses. For maximum effect, try a few raised beds with

thickly planted hybrid teas. Modern red brick walls can be a problem, so choose softer tones of yellow and pink. If you grow mixed borders, use other flowers and shrubs interplanted to give a longer flowering season. Make sure you know when the roses will flower and plan the rest of the garden accordingly.

Miniatures grow happily indoors and in window boxes. They need extra feeding, especially if they are planted in pots or small containers.

Clematis are perfect partners for a rose bush. They like the same sort of middle-rich soil and left alone will happily scramble through the branches to bloom on long after the roses have died away. Choose your combinations carefully; tones of blue, white and cream seem to blend best with pink and yellow roses.

SHAPES AND SIZES

There are as many kinds of rose bush as there are gardens. Starting from the top on the opposite page:

<u>Miniatures</u> – generally need little or no pruning, 1-1½ft.

<u>Bush</u> – the most popular shape for hybrid teas, which are grafted onto stock roots. Make sure the graft is above ground level or you will encourage suckers. Bushes need constant pruning to control growth; prune every winter as indicated by the two drawings on the bottom left; there should be three or four strong stems left. Prune above an outward facing bud, to make sure air and sunlight reach the middle.

<u>Floribundas, grandifloras, shrub and species</u> – allow to grow naturally, only cutting out deadwood, and weak or damaged branches.

<u>Standards</u> - used at the back of borders, or as a focal
point in a low bed; the second is a weeping shape.
Both are grafted onto a tall rose stock stem, and
must be supported with a stake all the time. Prune
as for hybrid tea bush, although the weeping
standard need not be cut back so drastically.
<u>Climber</u> - branching from the top of a stem. Prune
lightly to keep from getting too crowded.
<u>Rambler</u> - branching from the base, long and
straggly. Prune lightly, and tie low branches
down to encourage flowering.

ROSES TO GROW

HYBRID TEAS

Christian Dior: crimson double blossom 2-4½ ft

Etoile de Hollande: bright red, double blossom, very fragrant 2½-4 ft

Fragrant Cloud: coral red, double blossom more than 4ft

Pascali: creamy white double over 4ft

Peace: yellow-pink, pointed buds open into double flowers

FLORIBUNDAS

Iceberg: double white, pink at center 6-8ft

Lilac Charm: lilac, single 2-3ft

GRANDIFLORAS

Queen Elizabeth: medium, double, the original grandiflora, introduced 1954 4-6 ft

Pink Parfait: pale pink, double 2½-4ft

HYBRID PERPETUALS

<u>American Beauty</u>: vivid red, double, strong fragrance 4-5 ft

<u>Frau Karl Druschki</u>: white, double, blooms continuously 4-6 ft

<u>Reine des Violettes</u>: mauve, flat double, strong fragrance 5-8 ft

OLD SHRUB ROSES

<u>Cardinal de Richelieu</u>: violet, double 4-6 ft

<u>Gloire de Guilan</u>: clear pink, double, a damask rose, strong fragrance, historically used for making attar in Persia, 3-5 ft

<u>Fantin-Latour</u>: pink, flat double, a cabbage rose, rounded bushes 4-6 ft

<u>Buff Beauty</u>: creamy yellow, double, spreading bushes 4-6 ft wide and tall

Souvenir de la Maison :	pink, semi-double (a China rose) strong fragrance 2-3 ft blooms continuously

MODERN SHRUB ROSES AND SPECIES

Blanc Double de Coubert :	white, double, strong fragrance 5-7 ft
Fruhlingsgold :	yellow, single blossom fragrant, with large red hips 5-7 ft
Max Graf :	pink blossom with gold centers, single, unusually low, thickly growing, excellent ground cover
Nevada :	white, single blossom 5-8 ft
Rosa Rubrifolia :	tiny pink, single, purple red leaves used in arrangements, blooms once a year, 5-7 ft

<u>Rosa Moyesii</u> :	deep red and pink, single, 6~8 ft with magnificent hips
MINIATURES	
<u>Bo-Peep</u> :	tiny double pink blossoms 5~8 inches
<u>Twinkles</u> :	white, double blossom 8-10 in.
CLIMBERS	
<u>American Pillar</u> :	red with white centers, single 15~20 ft
<u>Golden Showers</u> :	daffodil yellow, double, blooms continuously 6-12 ft nearly thornless
<u>New Dawn</u> :	blush pink, double, blooms continuously 15~20 ft
<u>Zephirine Drouhin</u> :	bright pink, semi-double very fragrant, sometimes called the thornless rose

HERALDIC SYMBOLS

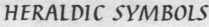

> Richard Plantagenet: If he suppose that I
> have pleaded truth
> From off this brier pluck
> a White rose with me.
>
> Shakespeare

The rose was a popular heraldic seal, used by numerous popes and royal families over the centuries, but nowhere was it more significant than in England. The first Earl of Lancaster brought the Red Rose from France to England in the thirteenth century as his emblem. His own brother, Edward I, was the first, but hardly the last English sovereign to employ a Golden Rose as his device.

The War of Roses (1445–1487) is probably the most famous floral contest in history.

In the scene imagined by Shakespeare, set in London's Temple Gardens, the Lancastrians reaffirm their use of the Red Rose device, after Richard of York chooses White. Only after years of bitter fighting does peace come at last with the marriage between Henry VII and Elizabeth of York to seal the new royal inheritance. The Red and White flowers were incorporated into the famous Tudor Rose.

Henry VIII's wives, Katherine of Aragon, Anne Boleyn, Jane Seymour and Katherine Parr all used the flower on their badges, and it is still today part of the royal coat of arms.

FAMILY TREE

A family tree is also a form of heraldry - a visual symbol of personal history, an emblem for reminding children and grandchildren of their roots and the branches tying the family together.

So, here is a Family Tree to fill in. Begin at the top with the youngest children and trace back to the first members you know about. If you have many more relatives than there are labels, copy the tree onto a larger sheet of paper, and let it expand. Decorate it with a border from another page, or paint the flowers and leaves in the rose tones you think appropriate for each individual. You will have an unusual and lovely addition to your family records.

QUILTING PARTIES

Twas from Aunt Dinah's quilting party
I was seeing Nellie home ....

Stephen Foster

Quilting has a long history; even in ancient Egypt and China warm winter clothes were a necessity. But the art of quiltmaking was especially strong in Colonial America, when the women gathered for Quilting Bees in the spring of the year to talk, sew, and gossip.

To protect its own textiles, England had made it illegal for the colonies to make their own cloths. Saving every scrap of used material became a patriotic act for the rebellious pioneers, and the early random designs were called scrap quilts. Patterns reflected the natural world ~ shells, birds, stars, and of course, flowers. There were regional variations: Philadelphia and Boston were the source of elegant medallion designs, Quaker patterns were cool and simple.

You can make a quilt for yourself which will be
an heirloom for your family. Using left-over scraps
from a summer dress or a baby smock, you will have
your own Memory Quilt, a souvenir of a happy
past made for the future.

40

MAKING A ROSE QUILT

The patterned pieces on the opposite page are for a Rose of Sharon design to make in square blocks. For a single bed coverlet you will need 77 ten-inch squares, seven across, eleven long, with a one-inch binding all round.

Cut out the squares from your fabrics, using shades of pink and green to blend with your decorating scheme. For each background square you will also need: one of each circle, four of the straight stems and buds, eight of the curved stems and buds, and eight leaves. Tack three graduated circles together through their middles. Then tack lightly to the exact middle of a square. Pin the flowers in place, and sew each piece down, using a buttonhole or satin stitch as shown. Follow the design on page 39, top left, for accuracy.

Finally, hem all the blocks together. Press flat, add a contrasting binding all the way around, and back with a non-slip matching cotton.

41

ATTAR OF ROSE

When the Mogul Emperor of Persia was married, he filled a garden canal with rosewater. As the newly-married couple strolled along the bank, they saw oil had formed on the surface. When it was collected, the sweet fragrance was so enchanting the bride named it Atar Jehangiri, or "Perfume of Jehan Ghir" after her husband.

Today attar is made in Bulgaria, India and France; they use the Cabbage and Damask roses, and the hybrid Ulrich Brunner. The flowers are picked and dis-tilled on the same day to conserve the precious oil ~ it takes 60,000 roses to make just one ounce of attar.

Below are instructions from <u>The Bengal Dispensatory</u> for making attar; this method was used in 1842.

"The Roses are put into the still, and water passes over gradually,...the Rose-water is placed in a large metal basin, covered with wetted muslin, tied over to prevent insects or dust getting into it; this vessel is let into the ground, which has been previously wetted with water. Attar is always made...while nights are cool; in the morning, the film formed upon the surface during the night, is removed by means of a feather, carefully placed in a small phial; as the collection is made, it is placed for a short period in the sun; and after a sufficient quantity has been procured, it is poured off clear, and of the colour of amber, into small phials."

POT-POURRI

The tiny leftovers from quiltmaking were often used for pot-pourri bags, filled with dry petals, spices and preservatives. Dry pourri also looks attractive, so pile it into open bowls, and stir to release the scent as you pass.

<u>Basic Directions.</u>

Roses and other flowers for pot pourri should be picked when the blossoms are just about to open and after the morning dew has evaporated. Then place the petals on muslin, cotton, or net curtain fabric stretched over boxes or frames. Allow to dry thoroughly. In the sun, drying is quick, yet essential oils can be lost. Room drying takes longer (up to five days), but does retain the oils. The petals should be turned over on the second day.

Almost all recipes combine one part leaves with seven of petals. The best roses are the old fashioned Apothecary's rose, the Damask and Cabbage, or Zephyrine Drouhin and Fragrant Cloud. Roses grown in well mulched soil have a stronger scent. Blend the petals with carnations, pansies, violets, or any highly perfumed but non-fleshy flowers. Add herbs such as rosemary or lavender, and tiny whole rosebuds for the open bowl. Spices to use include cloves, nutmeg, and lemon peel.

Preservatives and fixatives: dried and ground angelica root, cassia buds, clary seeds, powdered orris root, sandalwood, and dried woodruff.

THE LANGUAGE OF ROSES

I sent thee late a rosy wreath,
Not so much honouring thee
As giving it a hope that there
It could not wither'd be;
But thou thereon didst only
breathe
And sent'st it back to me;
Since when it grows, and
smells, I swear
Not of itself but thee!
                    Ben Jonson

The various types and shades of roses have distinctive symbolic meanings in what is known as "rose language". When sending roses, you can select the most appropriate one, based upon its special meaning –

American Beauty Rose   True, sincere love
Austrian Copper Brier   You are all that is lovely

Cabbage rose (Rosa centifolia)	Ambassador of love
Cherokee rose	Indian love song
China rose	Grace and beauty always new
Damask rose	Bashful love
Dog rose (Rosa canina)	Pleasure mixed with pain
Général Jacqueminot	I am true
Japanese rose (Rosa rugosa)	Beauty is your only attraction
Maiden's Blush rose	If you love me you will discover it
Maréchal Niel	Yours, heart and soul
Moss rose	Superior merit; voluptuous love
Musk rose	Capricious beauty
Pompom miniatures	Gentility, prettiness
Provence roses	My heart is in flames

A NOSEGAY

They are not long, the days of wine and roses:
    Out of a misty dream
Our path emerges for a while, then closes
    Within a dream.

               Ernest Dowson

The tear down childhood's cheek that flows
    Is like a dewdrop on the rose;
When next the summer breeze comes by,
    And waves the bush, the flower is dry.

               Sir Walter Scott

Each Morn a Thousand Roses brings, you say;
Yes, but where leaves the Rose of Yesterday?

               Omar Khayyám

49

FOR VALENTINE'S DAY

Here's a Valentine. Trace the heart pattern from the Valentine card on the opposite page onto a piece of cardboard and then cut it out.

Next, cut out the same shape from ½-inch-thick foam rubber. Put the foam on top of the cardboard and cover both with red velvet, taping the fabric evenly to the back of the card or gluing it tightly.

Take a piece of art board, white on both sides. Fold it down the middle. This is your basic card. Paste the bottom side onto a rectangular paper doily. Cover the doily on the back of the card with a thin sheet of red paper. Glue the velvet heart onto the front of the card, decorate the remaining space with curlicues and border patterns as shown. Glue a ribbon to the back, thread through two slits and tie at the front in a bow.

I Love You

SWEETER THAN ROSES

One of the most delightful forms of rose cookery is making candied rose petals for decorating desserts of all kinds. This culinary art probably dates from Roman times and certainly by the sixteenth century it became one of the most fashionable ways of adding a touch of artistry to the sweet part of the meal. The French were particularly fond of crystallized fruits and flowers.

Old French recipes travelled to the New World via the French-speaking settlers of Louisiana. The following is originally from New Orleans.

Crystallized Rose Petals

4 cups fresh stemmed violets or whole rosebuds
2 cups granulated sugar
1 cup hot water

Wash, stem and drain flowers, being careful not to bruise the petals. In a saucepan dissolve the sugar thoroughly in the hot water. Add the flowers. Put over medium heat and let the syrup simmer until a drop of syrup reaches the soft ball stage in cold water. Stir the flowers gently with a wooden spoon. Remove from heat and continue to stir gently until the syrup begins to granulate and reaches the consistency of coarse meal. Empty the contents over a wire rack or into a colander and shake off the excess sugar. Cool and pack the flowers in jars. Seal. Use as decoration or serve in little cut glass compotes.

Among the rose's virtues was its healing quality. Honey of roses was reputed by Gerarde to cure "ulcers and old wounds".

Honey of Roses

Cut the white heels from Red Roses and discard, take half a pound of them and put them into a stone jar, and pour on them three pints of boiling water. Stir well and let them stand twelve hours. Then press off the liquor, and when it has settled, add to it five pounds of honey. Boil it well, and when it is of the consistence of thick syrup it is ready to put away.

A modern version....

½ pound sweet pink or red rose petals
½ pound strained honey
Water
Juice of one lemon

Pick the petals from fresh sweet roses gathered after the dew has dried off. Measure the honey in a cup. For each cup of honey, add one cup of water. Mix honey, water, and rose petals and boil until flowers are tender. Strain the syrup into a saucepan. Pour the petals into hot sterilized jelly glasses. Return the syrup to the heat and cook until it begins to jell. Add lemon juice and bring back once to boiling. Remove from heat and pour over the rose petals to fill the glasses. Cool. Seal with paraffin. This is a delicate preserve that has a faint pink tint and light fragrance.

A very different dish to refresh the appetite.

Siamese Salad

2 full-blown roses	¼ pound cooked, diced pork
2 tablespoons soy sauce	6 cooked, diced shrimp
2 tablespoons lemon juice	2 tablespoons salad oil
1 teaspoon sugar	1 clove garlic, crushed
1 tablespoon chopped peanuts	½ cup minced onions
Salt	Lettuce leaves

Remove petals from roses and cut into small pieces. Combine soy sauce, lemon juice, sugar, peanuts, salt. Add rose petals, pork and shrimp. Place mixture on fresh lettuce leaves. Brown the garlic and minced onions in small frying pan. Pour hot on top of salad and serve immediately.

This 19th century lip salve was made more pleasant to use because of the rose ingredients.

Rose Lip Salve

1 lb oil of almonds, ½ lb white wax, ½ oz alkanet root. Melt and digest until sufficiently coloured, strain, and when cool, add a little water of roses.

THE SECRET FLOWER

Secrecy has always been connected with roses, ever since the Romans believed that Cupid dedicated the rose to Harpocrates, God of silence, as a bribe to be quiet about his mother's indiscretions. It was an appropriate gift because the petals cover the stamens in the same way that lips cover the mouth. At banquets fresh roses were hung from the ceilings to encourage guests to show the same discretion as Harpocrates; nothing should be repeated that was said 'under the rose' or sub rosa. Centuries later, plasterwork roses served the same purpose, and one of the loveliest examples is carved on the colonnades of the Piazza della Signoria in Florence. As always, the Church adapted useful pagan symbols and roses were placed on the tops of confessionals to guarantee privacy — Pope Hadrian gave permission for wooden carvings to take the place of the fresh flowers.

The Syrians used the rose as an emblem of immortality

as did the Chinese and Greeks who carved it on their tombs.

By the 18th century, the rose was used for more secular secrets. Scottish and English royalists who continued to fight for the Stuart dynasty drank a toast to "The King Over The Water"~the exiled James II and his descendants living in France, James Edward Stuart, and his son Bonnie Prince Charlie. Their Jacobite glasses were often engraved with a full-blown rose for James, and its bud which stood for Prince Charlie.

Nonetheless, the rose wasn't always a Stuart symbol. At Lullingstone Castle in Kent, the old Roman tradition was revived. A rose medallion nearly two feet in diameter decorated the ceiling, surrounded by this inscription:

Kentish True Blue,
Take this as a token,
That what is said here,
Under the rose is spoken.

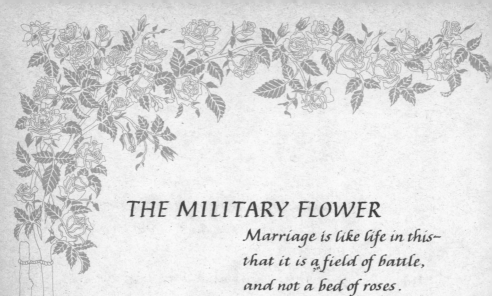

THE MILITARY FLOWER

> *Marriage is like life in this—*
> *that it is a field of battle,*
> *and not a bed of roses.*
>
> *R.L. Stevenson*

Prince Charles Edward's Highlanders wore white roses in their bonnets when they marched into England in 1745.

King George II's soldiers wore white roses at the Battle of Minden in 1759.

During the Indian wars in Florida, a Mrs. Grant was killed by the Seminole. It's said a rose grew where her blood stained the earth and it was named the Grant Rose.

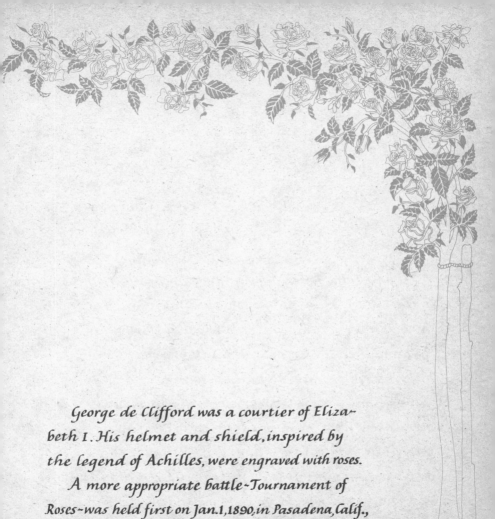

George de Clifford was a courtier of Elizabeth I. His helmet and shield, inspired by
the legend of Achilles, were engraved with roses.
    A more appropriate battle~Tournament of
Roses~was held first on Jan.1, 1890, in Pasadena, Calif.,
now the day of the Rose Bowl football game.

RING O'ROSES

Ring-a-ring o'roses
A pocket full of posies
A-tishoo! A-tishoo!
We all fall down.

Roses stand for many things, some pleasant, others less so. The nursery rhyme which children sing dates back to the days of the Plague. A rosy rash was followed by sneezing, then the victims all falling down.

This ring o'roses is a happier symbol ~ use it in miniature for a doll, in a larger size for the dining table, or a headdress for a young bridesmaid.

<u>Materials Required</u>:

Red and green satin ribbon, 1 cm (½ in.) wide; 14 artificial leaves; stem and binding wires; green tape and glue.

Turn over the top of a wire stem, and bind it to form a hook. Cut a piece of red satin ribbon 5 cm (2 in.) long, and bind to the end of the stem. Twist the ribbon to form a long coil. Bring back the loose ends onto the stem and secure with binding wire. Cut off any remaining ribbon and cover the wire with green tape. Use up all the ribbons in the same way, to make red and green flowers. Use ready-made cloth leaves or make your own from non-fraying cloth glued to wires. Twist all the stems together like a miniature daisy chain, adding flowers and leaves alternately, and join up to make a tiny ring.

1.   2.   3.   4.   5.

MUSICAL NOTES

> The fragrant kisses too, which I
> gathered by night
> From the rose-bush of your lips...
>
> J. Brahms

Folk songs and ballads bring wild roses to life, classical lieder mourn dolefully about roses and death, waltzes from Vienna whirl in our hearts as heady and dazzling as the scent of armfuls of hothouse American Beauties.

There are Rose Operas, too —The Rose of Castile (1857) by Balfe, and light-hearted operettas like Sir Arthur Sullivan's The Rose of Persia, which opened in 1899 at London's Savoy. But since its première in Dresden, Richard Strauss' Der Rosenkavalier has been performed more often than any other modern German opera. In the romantic opening scene of Act II, 17-year-old Octavian is sent by Baron Ochs to deliver a symbolic Silver Rose to the lovely young Sophia. Rose magic is more powerful than the Baron would like, and Octavian and Sophia fall in love.

Der Rosenkavalier is full of waltzes, reason enough for its popularity. Roses often inspire the nostalgia of home, with The Rose of Lucerne and Rose of the Alps, the Yellow Rose of Texas or The Rose of Tralee. Since World War I they've been shining in Picardy, and we all regret our own "days of wine and roses." There are sad songs (remember that red roses are for blue ladies) and happy ones too: when Ethel Merman came to the front of the stage in 1959 in Gypsy, she held out her arms and that clear voice told all of New York that everything's coming up roses!

THE SPIRIT OF THE DANCE

Oh, raise your deep-fringed lids that close
To wrap you in some sweet dream's thrall;
I am the spectre of the rose
You wore but last night at the ball.

Théophile Gautier

In the world of ballet, the rose often makes a symbolic appearance. During the second act of The Sleeping Beauty, Aurora and her four suitors dance the lovely and beautiful Rose Adagio. Each suitor gives her two roses as symbols of eternal love, but she hands the flowers teasingly to her mother instead.

The rose actually comes alive in Le Spectre de la Rose (inspired by the Gautier poem quoted above). A young girl returns from her first ball, carrying a rose as a souvenir of the evening's magic. She falls asleep holding it next to her cheek, as the Rose Spirit flies in through her window. They dance together in a dream, reliving the glorious excitement of the evening. Finally, the girl sinks back into her chair, and the Spirit flies out of the window, leaving her to awaken still holding her precious rose.

First produced by the revolutionary Ballet Russe de Monte Carlo in 1911, and staged by Diaghilev, Spectre was created by Fokine for Nijinsky - the first great ballet solo for a male dancer. Leon Bakst designed the costume - hundreds of silk petals sewn to a transparent base, covering the body with shifting iridescent pinks like Tiffany glass. On the first night, the incomplete costume had to be pinned in place, and Nijinsky must have felt very much like a rose among the thorns.

A FEW MORE RECIPES

The Damask rose has been the type most frequently used since ancient days for perfume. Today in France, rose oil is made also from Rose de Mai, a hybrid of Rosa centifolia and Rosa gallica.

King Edward VI Perfume

Take twelvespoonsful of bright red rose water, the weight of six pense in fine powdered sugar and boyle it on hot embers and coals softly, and the house will smell as though it were full of Roses. But you must burn the Sweet Cypress wood before to take away the gross ayre.

The Queen's Closet Opened, 1655

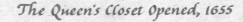

Swedish Rose Hips Soup

2 cups (1½ lb) dried rose hips   Water

½ cup raw sugar or honey to taste

Whipped cream   Slivered almonds

Crush or grind the rose hips and place in a saucepan with one and one-half quarts water. Bring to a boil, cover and simmer 45 minutes, stirring occasionally.

Strain through a fine sieve. Measure liquid and return to the saucepan. Add enough water to make liquid up to one and one-half quarts. Add sugar or honey. Mix arrowroot with small amount of water and add to rose hips liquid. Heat, stirring, until mixture thickens. Cover and chill. Serve cold with garnish of whipped cream and slivered almonds.

Rosewater drinks and sherbets were once sold in Egyptian streets by vendors who carried huge glass flasks strapped to their backs and metal cups for their customers. The rose syrup was supposed to bring health and beauty to all who drank it regularly.

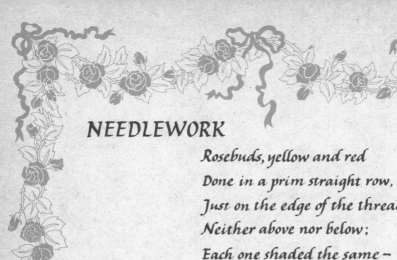

NEEDLEWORK

Rosebuds, yellow and red
Done in a prim straight row,
Just on the edge of the thread,
Neither above nor below;
Each one shaded the same –
With all the art that she knew–
Making her cross-stitched name,
Ann Elizabeth Drew.

Unknown

As soon as strips of bark or woven cloth began
to be sewed together, the decorative element became
as important as the function. Seams were tied
with bright wools and double knots, and laces were
made with ribbons and beads. When textiles

could be made in larger pieces, needlework became even more freely used. The petalled, round rosette is one of the oldest motifs in folk art, and it has been found on Egyptian grave cloths, Cherokee blankets, Middle Eastern rugs, and Scandinavian lace – just a few of the many examples there for the interested needleworker to use as inspiration.

We have chosen three kinds of embroidery for you to copy: a sampler, easy enough for a child to make in cross-stitch; a crewel rose, and a more elaborate tapestry flower and stem.

A CROSS-STITCH SAMPLER

Samplers were originally made by embroiderers as scrapbooks, with patterns copied from books. By the 16th century, needlewomen kept one piece of cloth as a notebook, and bits of embroidery were organised into strips with carefully arranged stitches. Lacemakers made runners, changing pattern to show off their skill. Soon, salesmen began to carry samplers, showing what could be made with the goods, and bringing the latest fashions to villages. Girls learning to sew were given stitches to copy, and it became a challenge to mix stitches and motifs together. By the Victorian period, the stereotyped designs had become dull and uninteresting, but this century has seen a revival of interest in making new and imaginative samplers with individual and often intentionally humorous themes.

Use the basic model opposite as a starting point, then add borders, trellis work and corner decorations adapted from the drawings on other pages.

A CREWEL ROSE

Early crewel embroideries had brilliantly patterned, full-blooming flowers. The Elizabethans filled rooms with embroidery running riot over every inch of cloth. American crewel was simpler. Wool was scarce and dyes were usually indigo blue. Today we combine the best of both, allowing space around each figure so it shows up against the background, yet using bright shades of modern wools for interest.

The crewel rose can be a cushion or border for curtains and bedspreads. Trace the outline onto the right side of the cloth, then fill in with a simple long and short stitch. Use pinks or reds or, more dramatically, copy shadings of newer hybrids, in apricot or coral, or try the contrast of pure white crewel wool on sheer white organdy. Remember to work with a frame, so the fabric will not pucker.

73

A TAPESTRY FLOWER

Needlepoint is more fun when you make your own designs. This graph makes it easy to count out the stitches on unmarked canvas. Use it for a simple rose on 14-point canvas for a petit-point eyeglass case, on 10-point canvas for a decorative panel. Trace the flower onto paper for an outline, cut out two shapes, simply reverse one from left to right and you have a pair of roses for appliqué!

Embroider squares of 14-point canvas, then sew them all together to make a beautiful rose carpet.

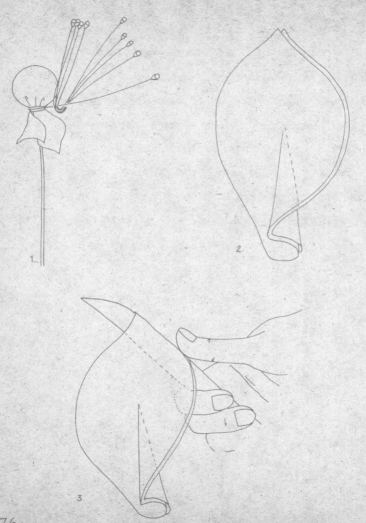

1.

2.

3.

ORGANDY ROSE

Wreathe a straw hat with these beautifully blowsy flowers. Make a soft ball on top of a wire stem and bind in place. Fold yellow-painted wire in half, thread each with a yellow bead, hooking the wire over to keep the bead in place. Sew down as shown. Cut out two layers of a petal shape in organdy or organza, fold at the base and tack into place around the ball. Make up four more petals, tack down and bind at the top of the stem with green ribbon. Curl each petal slowly over the back of a knife. Sew onto the hat, or onto a ribbon tied around the crown.

ROSE LORE

The Classic Flower

The Egyptian enchantress, Mythris, asked to be buried in a rose embroidered cloak and her tomb was filled with rose petals and flowers.

Epicurus (341-271 B.C.) had a rose garden made for himself in Athens so he would always have fresh flowers. Another Roman story said that the guests of Heliogabalus were accidentally (some say intentionally) suffocated by the stifling perfume of an overabundant rose banquet.

The Egyptians created the first artificial roses by cutting petals from thin wood chips which were then dyed red and scented with rose oil. Pliny tells us that later on they made roses from cloth and paper for exportation to Greece and Rome.

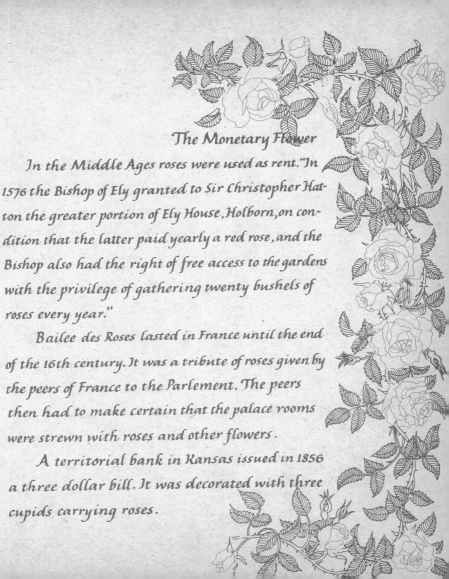

The Monetary Flower

In the Middle Ages roses were used as rent. "In 1576 the Bishop of Ely granted to Sir Christopher Hatton the greater portion of Ely House, Holborn, on condition that the latter paid yearly a red rose, and the Bishop also had the right of free access to the gardens with the privilege of gathering twenty bushels of roses every year."

Bailee des Roses lasted in France until the end of the 16th century. It was a tribute of roses given by the peers of France to the Parlement. The peers then had to make certain that the palace rooms were strewn with roses and other flowers.

A territorial bank in Kansas issued in 1856 a three dollar bill. It was decorated with three cupids carrying roses.

Rose nobles were created for the York kings: Edward IV issued the first in 1465, commemorating a sea victory. It replaced the noble first issued in 1346. With a flower on the ship's side, it was valued at 10s and was issued until 1470. Another coin was issued by Henry VIII, with the Tudor emblem. King James' rose noble bore a rose on one side and a thistle on the other.

Around the World

Rosewood, from Brazil, a beautifully figured wood, is named for the rose-like scent of its flowers.

The Persians say the nightingale cries whenever a rose is picked.

Instead of plucking daisies, an old Georgian wives' tale says if you fold a rose in half and it splits your love is returned, if not – not.

In Germany falling rose petals are a sign of death.

At the Sèvres porcelain factory, Rose Pompadour, a unique enamel glaze, was named after the Marquise de Pompadour in 1764.

And, as a truly international flower, "La Rose Malade", inspired by William Blake, was created for Maya Plisetskaya, of the Bolshoi Ballet. Costumes were by Yves St. Laurent, choreography by Roland Petit, to music by Gustav Mahler.

THE COLLECTOR'S ROSE

Unger Bros. of Newark, New Jersey, made many of the small silver pieces popular around the turn of the century.

Tea sets were made in a simple rose design, berry bowls had handles of wild roses and the Queen of Flowers' dressing table set had a nude figure in the Art Nouveau style surrounded by entwined roses.

Birds and roses were combined again in a pattern made by the Alvin Company called Bridal Rose. They also made a beautiful openwork spoon with a rose bowl.

From the 18th century onwards, you will find enamel patch boxes, with roses entwined with doves and a sentimental motto, or a single full-blown rose. They were made in England and France.

Transfer-printed little pots
from Staffordshire, England, were
decorated with rose bouquets and
wreaths, often around a perfumer's
name. These were very popular
between 1840 and 1890.

Engine-turned designs of the
1920's from the workshops of
Cartier and Tiffany were covered
in pale enamels and decorated
with tiny rosebuds at the corners.

Limoges, Dresden and Sèvres
porcelain dresser sets were well-
known in Europe for their hand-

painted rose medallions. In England,
Coalport was particularly famous for
its naturalistic rose designs.

A modern Lenox pattern has a single
black rose, a reminder of its own long
floral tradition, and equally a pointer
for bottle collectors; The Rose family of
Atlanta, Georgia named their whiskey
after Rufus and Katie, husband and
wife, Randolph and Laura their
children. So Four Roses was created,
but one of their earliest jugs in 1870
now a rarity, featured a single black
rose.

EVERLASTING ROSES

Too many roses fade away ~ this one will stay forever. Plain pottery and porcelain was decorated at home by Victorian ladies. Ours is a modern interpretation. Trace the pattern onto transparent paper. Enlarge if necessary and prick along the outline with a thickish pin. Lay the paper on a plate and run over the outline with a soft charcoal pencil. Lift off the paper carefully and using special china or acrylic paints fill in according to the numbers suggested. Make six or eight in different shades for a very special dessert service.

1 PALE PINK

2 MEDIUM PINK

3 DARK PINK

4 RED

5 BROWN

6 PALE GREEN

7 MEDIUM GREEN

8 DARK GREEN

GREAT GARDENS TO VISIT

FRANCE

Besançon: Jardin Botanique

Chauvaniac: Château de
Lafayette

Evry-Petit-Bourg: Rosarium

Lyon: Jardin Botanique

Malmaison: Josephine's Gardens

Marseille: Jardin Botanique

Paris: Musée Rodin
Bagatelle
Roseraie de l'Hay

GERMANY

Frankfurt: Bethmannpark

Zweibrueken: Rosengarten

Baden-Baden: Lichtentaler
Allee

HOLLAND

The Hague: Peace Palace
Rosarium
Westbroekpark

BELGIUM

Ghent: Parc de la Citadelle

ITALY

Rome: Municipal Garden
Il Roseto all'
Aventino

SWITZERLAND

Geneva: Parc de la Grange

PORTUGAL

Oporto: Crystal Palace

DENMARK

Copenhagen: Valby Park

UNITED STATES	UNITED KINGDOM
Calif: San Francisco, Golden Gate Park Rose Garden	Aberdeen, Scotland: Drum Castle
Conn: Hartford, Elizabeth Park Rose Garden	Canterbury: Chilham Castle
Illinois: Chicago, Marquette Park Rose Garden	Cardiff, Wales: Roath Park
Iowa: Ames, Iowa State Univ. Rose Garden	Cranbrook: Sissinghurst Castle
New York: Ithaca, Cornell Univ. Rose Garden	London: Regent's Park, Queen Mary's Rose Garden
Brooklyn, Botanic Garden	Kew Gardens, Surrey
Penna: Hershey Rose Gardens	Loughborough: Prestwood Hall
Texas: Dallas, Samuell-Grand Municipal Rose Garden	Ripley: Wisley, Royal Horticultural Society
Virginia: Arlington Mem. Rose Gdn	**CANADA**
Washington, D.C.: Woodland Park Rose Garden	B.C.: Victoria, The Butchart Gardens
Washington: Seattle, Woodland Park Rose Garden	Quebec: Montreal, Connaught Park Rose Garden

ACKNOWLEDGEMENTS

Ada Gibson's _Receipt Book_, 1900

Allen-Gray, Dorothy - _Fare Exchange_
  Faber & Faber, 1963

An American, 1883 - _Ice-Cream and Cakes_-
  Charles Scribner's Sons, 1883

Botticelli's _The Birth of Venus_ - Uffizi
  Gallery, Florence

Brown, Marion - _Pickles and Preserves_ -
  Avenel Books, 1954

Cassell's Domestic Dictionary - Cassell,
  Patter, Galpin & Company

Cocteau Poster - Costume for
  Le Spectre de la Rose

Fantin-Latour - _Still Life_, 1866 - Washington
  D.C., Nat. Gallery of Art

Field, J - _Collecting Georgian & Victorian
  Crafts_ - Scribner's Sons, 1973

Gerarde, J - _Great Herball_, 1556

Hewitt, Jean - _The N.Y. Times Natural
  Foods Cookbook_ - Quadrangle Books 1971

McCall's Book of Quilts ~ Simon & Schuster, 1975

Papal Rose ~ Gold and Sapphires ~ 1562, Residenzmuseum, Munich

Rose gallica ~ _Minoan Fresco_ ~ Knossos, Crete

Rose Emblem ~ Tudor Choir Stall, Henry VII Chapel Westminster, London

The Rose of Tralee ~ N.Y., Red Star Music Company Inc.

Rose Windows ~ West Front of Chartres: Villa Maria Luisa, Milan

Sanecki, Kay M ~ _The Complete Book of Herbs_ ~ Macmillan 1974

Stafford & Ware ~ _Illustrated Dictionary of Ornament_ ~ St. Martin's, 1974 (German Ironwork)

Wilson, Marie M ~ _Siamese Cookery_ ~ Charles E. Tuttle, 1965

92

BOOKS TO READ

Bunyard, Edward A. *Old Garden Roses*.
    Scribner's, 1937
Culpeper, Nicholas. *The Complete Herbal*.
    British Directory Office, 1649
Foster-Melliar. *The Book of Roses*.
    Macmillan, 1894
Hole, Dean S. *A Book About Roses*.
    Edward Arnold, 1870
Redouté, P. J. *Les Roses*.
    Didot, 1817
Thomas, Graham S. *Old Shrub Roses*.
    Phoenix House, 1963
Thomson, Richard. *Old Roses for Modern Gardens*.
    Van Nostrand, 1959

INDEX